MONEY, MEN *and* MACHINES

MONEY, MEN
and MACHINES

BY
WADDILL CATCHINGS
AND
CHARLES F. ROOS

Duell, Sloan and Pearce · *New York*
Little, Brown and Company · *Boston*

LIBRARY OF CONGRESS CATALOG CARD NO. 53-6448

FIRST EDITION

DUELL, SLOAN AND PEARCE—LITTLE, BROWN
BOOKS ARE PUBLISHED BY
LITTLE, BROWN AND COMPANY
IN ASSOCIATION WITH
DUELL, SLOAN & PEARCE, INC.

*Published simultaneously
in Canada by McClelland and Stewart Limited*

PRINTED IN THE UNITED STATES OF AMERICA

Foreword

Money, Men and Machines has been written for four essential reasons:

1. To make clear that the Federal Government, in managing the stream of our circulating money, exercises vast powers over the daily economic life of the United States.

2. To show that our officials today, in exercising these regulatory powers, are interfering with the successful operation of our economic machinery.

3. To state why our economic leadership is taking us away from economic freedom, and toward more and more Government control of economic life.

4. To suggest a new objective of monetary control which will enable America to maintain a high level of employment and production by avoiding the great increases and decreases in the supply of money that cause booms and depressions.

The authors believe that the most dangerous threat to our freedom, either from within or without, lies in our confusion of thought concerning our supply of money. The fear of inflation is one of the most powerful forces in our daily life. Congress, influenced by public opinion, passes law after law in an effort to protect the value of the dollar.

Meanwhile, almost all Americans, no matter how well informed on other aspects of our national life, are confused and misled on the subject of money. This situation is as tragic as it is needless, since all the knowledge the public requires about the causes of inflation and the methods of prevention may be easily acquired.

In fact, the authors believe that it can be learned

with no more difficulty than subjects which are taught in elementary school, such as geography and arithmetic. And it is their hope that when you have finished this book, you will readily agree with them.

WADDILL CATCHINGS
CHARLES F. ROOS

January 5, 1953
New York City

Contents

MONEY, MEN *and* MACHINES

I

This Is Our System

THE PRE-EMINENT POSITION of the United States in the world today, and the high standard of living of our people, are the direct results of competitive enterprise. For more than three centuries our men and women have freely followed their own pursuits and, by their initiative and ingenuity, have built up a vast productive power.

We have more and better tools than other nations; we make greater use of electricity, steam and oil; we apply more effectively our skills and know-how; and we have developed marvelous methods of mass production. Further, we produce with much less effort than other people. That is why an hour of work in the United States today will buy far more than an hour of work anywhere else in the world.

That is why, in relation to other countries, we Americans have more food, clothes, houses, plumbing, cars, telephones, radios, TV sets, iceboxes, washing machines and hundreds of other conveniences in everyday life; more in medical and hospital facilities; more opportunities for education and culture; more time for sheer recreation and entertainment. All this has been accomplished by our system of competitive enterprise.

Through daily competition we develop and use new ideas, improve our machines, extend our production and put diligent and decisive people in charge of all kinds of activities. Adventurous men and women in every field of industry, commerce, finance and agriculture are always seeking ways to supply what buyers want, for they know that the cash register is a kind of ballot box which automatically gets rid of the ineffectual and incompetent.

Our American production is based on teamwork extending throughout our whole economic life. By this teamwork, materials are gathered from all over the earth and divided among an amazing variety of products, which are fashioned by millions of men and women and then delivered for sale to buyers everywhere. Even those people who produce something for themselves get help from others, since they use materials or tools, seeds or chemicals, supplied by the work of thousands of other men and women.

And yet, no matter how plentiful our raw materials and labor supply, how wonderful our factories, how fertile our fields, we must have one more vital ingredient for actual production. That is money — plain dollars and cents. Without it, all our talents, all our tools, would be useless.

Money is not merely a matter of convenience — a medium of exchange. It is an instrument of progress and growth. In our world today, its circulation is the stimulating current that activates the economic life of 158,000,000 Americans.

Everybody works for money in our teamwork

[5]

system of production — the manual worker, the brain worker and the capitalist are all paid for the parts they play. Wages, salaries, rent, interest, profits and dividends are rendered in money. This provides income, and with the income we buy food, clothing, shelter, medical attention, entertainment and all other goods and services. As producers we receive and use money for production, and as consumers we receive and use money for consumption.

In short, when you combine money with men and machines, you have the three essentials to a healthy economy. It is this combination which permits us to keep going and reap the rewards of our competitive-enterprise system.

Who Does the Planning?

Under competitive enterprise, our planning is done mostly by the businessmen who conduct our productive activities. It is true, of course, that as we consumers buy things, we plan in effect for more

[6   ]

of those products; but the opportunity for the individual to make a selection is provided by business planning. Improved goods and services, new equipment and methods and processes, more production or less production — our whole economy is given pace and direction by the decisions made by businessmen.

This planning is always guided by the twin factors of prices and profits. As prices move up and down, each businessman watches those which concern his own activities, and weighs their effect upon his profit-making opportunities. In this way, the price-and-profit mechanism of teamwork production relates the plans of each individual to the plans of all other individuals.

Proof of this lies in the vast network of interwoven prices which extends through all our fields of industry, commerce and agriculture. Although the products are almost limitless in grades, qualities and styles, each has a price at each stage of production, and each price is related to other prices.

[7   ]

Any individual price movement affects the status of other prices, and thus influences the possibilities of profit or loss.

However, despite the changes that occur constantly, the American businessman is readily able to keep our productive machinery working in harmony. Indeed, production as we know it in the United States would be impossible were it not for the operation of this simple but effective price-and-profit mechanism.

Five Keys to Production

Changing prices perform five basic functions in our highly organized teamwork production.

1. They keep us informed of shifts in the relation between supply and demand. They reflect past, present and prospective increases or decreases in supply or demand (unless production is restrained by monopoly or Governmental control). They are our only means of learning the facts about our

enormous and complicated economic life. Even with masses of statistics and involved calculations, we cannot tabulate an endless series of sales, inventory and production records. But we promptly get the knowledge we need merely by observing the changes that occur in prices.

2. Changing prices are our medium for passing along to the consumer the aggregate cost of production. In this way we bring together the costs incurred in many different places as we produce with a widespread division of labor. Initial and intermediate costs, plus any price movements up or down at any stage of production, are reflected in the final price.

Intermediate movements may be due to methods, tools, transportation, wages, taxes or they may come merely from a change in supply or demand for a material or a partly finished product. But whatever the reason, or whenever or wherever the change occurs, the result is carried forward to be included as part of the ultimate purchase price.

[9]

3. By means of changing prices, we distribute our available supply among competing buyers. In a sense, the market in America's free society is an auction at which prospective purchasers bid for goods and services. Some bidders drop out as the price of a product goes up: some are unwilling or unable to pay more; some prefer to purchase something else.

But as prices go down, more and more people are able or willing to buy. In this way, our spending as buyers allows us, as producers, to apportion our output of goods and services.

Price movements, however, are caused not only by competition among buyers but also among sellers. The ingenious men and women who watch prices are always figuring costs and developing ideas. Eagerly they devise ways to offer products at lower prices, or of better quality.

The combined effect upon prices of these actions by producers and buyers is a unique and distinctive feature of our system of competitive enterprise.

4. Another function of changing prices is to direct the course of our economic life. Price movements provide the mechanism with which we stimulate, retard, control and guide all our productive activities.

Buyers raise the price of a product and thereby signal for more production; or they allow a price to drop, indicating that supply exceeds demand. Producers everywhere watch these figures as they make their plans on the basis of sales expectations.

5. Price movements, however, are not merely signals for more or less production. In themselves, they are powerful forces for actually increasing or decreasing production. That is because of their effect upon profit and loss, the other main element in our economic machinery.

By increasing profits, higher prices stimulate production in two ways. First, they permit higher-cost producers to engage in profitable operations. And second, they enable lower-cost producers to obtain more capital for more capacity and more output.

On the other hand, a downward movement of prices, by cutting profits or causing losses, brings about opposite results. Higher-cost producers are eliminated, and lower-cost operators divert some of their capital to other uses. Falling prices, therefore, are a force that keeps us from wasting our energies and piling up unwanted products.

Moreover, upward and downward price movements, by their effect upon profit and loss, guide us in distributing our raw and semifinished materials among America's multitudinous products. We determine how much of an available material to use for one purpose, and how much for another; or we calculate which of several materials to use when more than one is available.

For example, that is how we allocate steel for buildings, bridges, freight cars, razor blades; apportion corn for human food or animal food; or decide whether to use cotton, linen or nylon in automobile seat covers. That is how materials are gathered from around the globe and divided among an infinite variety of products which, when combined, give us the greatest outpouring of goods and services ever known to mankind.

The Power of Profits

Throughout all the operations of our economic machine, profits, especially high profits, are a strong force in achieving lower prices, more and better goods, new and improved services. The earnings go where they are most needed. They enable low-cost producers to increase their output and gain large markets at low prices. They supply the funds for extensive research by big companies like Ford, General Motors, General Electric — the kind of research that gives us such discoveries as television, radio, nylon and penicillin.

In competitive enterprise, there are always high profits for the more efficient producers. This is true

[13   ]

because costs vary while prices tend to be the same. Well-informed, thrifty buyers who are able to obtain a product at one price are not disposed to pay a higher price for the same thing.

Low-cost and high-cost producers, therefore, usually sell at much the same price. Consequently, when one person makes a "fair" or a "normal" profit, however these words may be defined, businessmen with more skill, initiative, or with superior production facilities will make more than the so-called fair or normal profit.

It is the plowing back of these profits for more and better production that provides 158,000,000 Americans with food, clothing and shelter, short hours of work, facilities for medical care, transportation, education, recreation, entertainment, and all the other things that comprise the highest standard of living in the civilized world.

The foregoing discussion relates to profits that result from the use of labor, tools and money in producing and distributing goods and services. Only these profits are part of our machinery of production, and perform the functions mentioned. There are profits, however, of another and entirely different kind: those that arise merely from owning something on which the price goes up without fabrication, transportation, storage, insurance, merchandising or other improvement between the time of purchase and the time of sale. These profits are not elements in our productive machinery; in fact, as we shall see, they actually interfere with its efficient operation by stimulating speculation.

Why We Have Depressions

W<small>E HAVE ALREADY OBSERVED</small> how businessmen, under the guidance of changing prices and profit or loss, organize our productive capacity to supply consumers' goods and services in the right proportions. However, this far-flung and intricate system is being changed almost daily to meet new methods and new tastes. For example, such changes as businessmen achieved when the automobile replaced the horse and buggy, or when such discoveries as radio and television appeared on the American scene.

Moreover, our economy is planned with so much flexibility and resilience that we can adjust easily to disturbances like unseasonal weather, disaster, crop failure and labor strikes. The vast area of our country, the great variety of our products, our superb credit and banking facilities, and our native resourcefulness allow us to overcome such difficulties without blocking the stream of money that circulates back and forth between ourselves as consumers and ourselves as producers.

We are equipped to do this because, when we are not able or required to make our regular purchases, we spend our money for something else. If there is a cool summer or a warm winter, the money we save on clothing goes into things like electrical appliances, furniture, or even a vacation trip. If a crop failure occurs, we buy other foods, or use materials from other fibers.

The result of this is that while some manufacturers and merchants have to carry unsold inventories from one season to the next, others enjoy unusually large sales. Hence, it might be said that what one group of producers loses, another group gains. And when such minor upsets occur, no general collapse follows.

In situations like these, our system of competitive enterprise is a powerful force for sustaining a high level of employment and production. Because some prices go up and some go down, because some profit-making chances are greater and some are less, our economic machine lets businessmen plan to make up in certain fields of activity what they have lost in others.

At the same time, payments on insurance, loans by banks, the forced use of hoarded money, and public and private welfare contributions — all add to the stream of money in circulation and tend to offset the withdrawals. In other words, our price and profit mechanism is quite capable of taking care of upsets caused by changing methods and tastes, or by natural disturbances.

However, there are other disturbances which affect not only groups of people but the whole of our economic life, and thus cripple our structure of business planning. These upsets, caused by great changes in our volume of circulating money, are the

[18]

result of loans and investments by commercial banks — the banks that carry checking accounts for the public.

Why do these changes in loans and investments play so vital a role in our economic life? Because, at certain times, huge sums in the aggregate are added to the stream, and at other times they are withdrawn. These fluctuations cause corresponding changes in the flow of money between consumers and producers. As the stream becomes larger, we spend more in almost every field of economic life; as the stream becomes smaller, we spend less.

When these fluctuations occur, our system of competitive enterprise does *not* function as a force for sustaining the level of employment and production. On the contrary, the price and profit mechanism actually directs our planning away from stability and toward the great ups and downs that we call booms and depressions.

In the early years of the nation, vast changes in our flow of money were caused by mining or the

[19]

import and export of gold, as well as by the print-ing and cancellation of paper currency. Today, they are caused primarily by increases or decreases in the loans and investments of commercial banks.

In fact, as will be shown later in this book, these loans and investments create the circulating bank deposits that *now constitute the main money supply of the United States!*

Impact upon Business Planning

When banks are increasing loans and invest-ments, businessmen make their plans with confi-dence and enterprise. Prices generally are strong, and profit-making possibilities are good. Manu-facturers and merchants build up their inventories or keep them at a level that helps production and trade. At the same time, they expand activity by building more plants and facilities, by adding to machinery and equipment.

But when banks are reducing their loans and investments, caution and anxiety take the place of confidence and enterprise. Upon the advice of bankers, the businessmen prepare for a decline in demand for their products and a weakening of prices; they postpone purchases and reduce inventories; they cut production and curtail plant expansion.

As a result, money flows slowly and at a low level throughout our channels of industry, commerce and agriculture. Our essential instrumentality fails to function, and across the country, the energizing force of America's economic life comes almost to a standstill.

Under this stress of violent money fluctuation, our price and profit mechanism works to make conditions worse instead of better. Since the stream of money affects all American business, virtually all prices are either strong or weak as the price level goes up or down. Likewise, the chances of making profits are generally either good or bad. In times of big production, business is stimulated toward still

[21   ]

more output; in times of stagnation common sense calls for less production.

But this is not all. When the price level is rising or falling, the chances for making speculative profits are good — in one case by buying in anticipation of higher prices, in the other by selling in the hope of buying later at lower prices.

But in either case, speculation is a powerful force in the wrong direction, and actually interferes with the successful operation of our productive machinery. Why? Because speculators add to demand when there is not enough supply, and add to supply when there is not enough demand.

Let's Look at History

As already indicated, great fluctuations in the flow of money are responsible for a correspondingly uneven level of activity in consumers' durable goods, in capital goods, and in the construction industries. Production in these fields comes in great waves or surges. Times of feverish production are followed by months or even years of relative stagnation and idleness.

America's economic history has been a succession of prosperous periods followed by the hard times of depression — big depressions such as occurred in 1837, 1857, 1873, 1893, 1907 and 1929; smaller ones such as those in 1920 and 1937; and little ones like that we recently went through in 1949. But in each case, one factor was clearly evident — a decreasing money supply.

No planning by businessmen can avoid the dire effects of such changes in our money supply. These changes result from the natural fact that people spend more when they receive more, and spend less when they have less. Therefore, the only way to get rid of these economic disturbances is to regulate the supply of money in such a manner as to keep our intricate economic machinery in efficient operation.

A Job for Government

We Americans live in what is called the Machine Age. By the use of machines, we lighten our labor in the factory and on the farm, in the home and on the road. Also, we use the power of electricity and other forces of nature to increase our industrial output, and to obtain more leisure time for education and recreation. And yet the rate at which we build machines goes up and down like a roller coaster, instead of like the steady upward advance of an escalator.

Are the monetary fluctuations that cause these booms and depressions inevitable? Indeed they are not. On the contrary, they are entirely within our control. But, first, our know-how about circulating money must match our know-how about engineering and production.

The first step toward gaining this knowledge is to recognize that control of the supply of money is a function of government — a basic fact that is just as true of our free-enterprise system as it is of any other system. By wise monetary management, our Federal Government can get rid of the great ups and downs in the flow of money, and let businessmen do their planning so as to create an expanding high level of production and employment.

Once our Government takes the proper steps for controlling the flow of money, we Americans should be able, with an even shorter work week, to increase sharply our output of goods and services. Then, every man and woman who is able and willing to work will achieve our long-sought-for goal of living a full life in comfort and security.

The Federal Reserve System

TODAY, the Government agency that has the responsibility of controlling our money supply is the Board of Governors of the Federal Reserve System. Established by Congress in 1935, the Board consists of seven members, appointed by the President and confirmed by the Senate. In numerous reports and pamphlets, and in the monthly *Federal Reserve Bulletin*, the Board makes clear its plans for regulating the supply, the availability, and the cost of money in the United States.

By law, the Board is empowered to control the ability of our commercial banks to lend and invest. These banks are allowed to increase their loans and investments — or are forced to decrease them —

only upon action by the Board. Therefore, in actuality, the huge fluctuations in our stream of circulating money are the result of decisions taken by the Federal Reserve governors.

As generally understood by Congress and the public, the purpose of the Board in controlling bank loans and investments is to prevent the creation of a supply of money out of proportion to our production of goods and services. That is what we call inflation — a condition that occurs when the amount of money in use is increased enough to cause a rise in the general price level (what we commonly call "the cost of living").

Actually, preventing inflation is only an objective of the Board that gets public attention. The Board's real purpose in managing our money will be discussed later. But before we do that, let us clearly understand what we use as money, how this money is created, and how the Board acts to prevent inflation by exercising control over commercial banks.

The Role of Circulating Deposits

Our money consists of coins, paper bills and circulating bank deposits. Since about 1860, our main money has consisted of circulating deposits.

More than 90 per cent of our payments are made by check; paper money and coins are used mostly for payrolls and small transactions. We deposit surplus cash in the bank, and draw checks from time to time to fulfill our needs in bills and coins.

Each month the *Federal Reserve Bulletin* calculates the amount of our money supply, as of a date about thirty days earlier. At the end of September 1952, we had about 164 billion dollars, consisting of more than 136 billion in deposit money, 27 billion in paper money, and from one to two billion in coin.

Under Federal law, deposit money, paper bills and coins are freely convertible, one into another. The Treasury Department furnishes the Federal Reserve banks with an ample supply of Reserve notes and coins, so as to provide commercial banks with as much currency as they need for check-cashing.

Reserve notes are obligations of the United States of America, as you may see by looking at one in your pocketbook. Today there are about 25 billion dollars of these in circulation, placed there by commercial banks in meeting the requirements of depositors.

Bank deposits are not unlike bank notes. Both are promises to pay, and both are used for making payments. The bank note is an engraved piece of paper, circulating from person to person; the bank deposit is an entry in an account book, circulating from person to person by means of checks and bookkeeping entries.

The "Creation" of Money

How bank loans and investments "create" money is shown by what happens when the Chase National lends a million dollars to the U. S. Steel Corporation. In making the loan, Chase credits the account of the Corporation with a million, and thereby creates a "deposit" against which U. S. Steel draws checks.

The setting up on the bank's books of this promise to pay brings into being a sum of money which did not exist before. The resulting increase is much the same as if the Chase National had printed and handed over to U. S. Steel a million dollars in bank notes.

Banks have been creating money this way ever since depositors began paying by check instead of by notes. Although this fact was not generally accepted until about twenty years ago, it had been known and understood for almost three centuries.

For instance, John Locke, a founder of the Bank of England, recorded his knowledge of the fact in 1692; Alexander Hamilton did the same in 1790; the Bank Commissioners of Massachusetts in 1860; and Professor Charles F. Dunbar of Harvard in 1899, in his *Theory and History of Banking*.

During the latter part of the ninteenth century and the early part of the twentieth, there was much argument among economists about the similarity between circulating notes and circulating deposits. The controversy continued until 1937, when James Harvey Rogers proved mathematically the amount of deposits that the commercial banks can create.

And thus we come to the situation as it exists in our country today. Because deposits are freely convertible into currency, the commercial banks in effect create notes and coins as well as deposit money. That is why the Federal Reserve System, in controlling bank loans and investments, actually controls the creation of the money supply in the United States.

Methods of Control

How THIS CONTROL is exercised is described by the Board in its official reports and publications. Three important methods are used:

1. Lowering or raising the discount rate — the amount a Reserve bank charges for making loans.
2. Permitting or forbidding commercial banks to make certain kinds of loans.
3. Manipulating what are known as "required reserves."

This latter banking expression has a strange meaning, but it must be understood if we want to know how the Board's monetary planning affects the planning of every American businessman. Perhaps the best way to understand the phrase is to see how it developed.

First, we must go back to 1863 and the passage of the National Bank Act — a law which required banks to carry in their vaults a percentage of cash as a reserve to pay depositors. The idea was simply to provide funds for the cashing of checks.

It turned out, however, that requiring a bank to maintain a specified reserve defeated the very purpose for which the reserve was created. Banks could not safely pay out what they were required to hold. The law, therefore, had the unexpected effect of immobilizing large amounts of cash in banks all over the country.

Consequently, in the Federal Reserve Act of 1913, Congress provided that the impounded cash be deposited in Reserve banks, and that, thereafter, the required reserves of a bank consist not of cash in the vault but of deposits with its Federal Reserve bank. In this way, twelve great regional pools of money were created, from which Reserve banks

[33   ]

were to lend currency to member banks to use in cashing checks.

Actually, the creation of these pools has proved to be relatively unimportant, since provisions of the Act covering issuance of Reserve notes enable the Reserve banks to obtain as much currency as they need for loans to member banks. But the fact that Reserve deposits serve as required reserves for member-bank deposits has proved to be of vital importance.

The reason for this is that required reserves set a limit to the amount of money a bank may create. Hence, Reserve bank deposits exercise a rigid control over the operations of our commercial banks.

To understand how this works, let us look again at the National Banking Act and its provisions for reserves. Take a bank that was required to have in its vaults cash equal to 25 per cent of its deposits, and say that this reserve amounted to ten million dollars. Therefore, the bank could have deposits of only forty million. And until it obtained more cash, it could create no more deposits.

Today, Reserve bank deposits perform the function that cash in the vault performed under the Banking Act. Thus, the bank mentioned above, with a 25 per cent reserve requirement, is limited to loans and investments which create deposits totaling no more than four times its Reserve bank deposits. To lend more than that, the bank must obtain more deposits with its Reserve bank.

Manipulation of Reserves

There are two ways in which the Board uses required reserves to control commercial bank loans and investments. The first is by increasing or decreasing the Reserve bank deposits that constitute the reserves. This is accomplished by causing the Reserve banks to increase or decrease the total of *their* loans and investments.

The result is a corresponding change in Reserve

[35   ]

bank deposits, since these institutions, like commercial banks, create deposits when they make loans and investments, and extinguish deposits when they receive payments.

The second way in which the Board uses required reserves as a method of control is by increasing or decreasing the *percentage* of reserves to be held by commercial banks. Under law, the Board has the power to set this percentage at any point between that prescribed in the Federal Reserve Act and twice that amount. For example, the statutory percentage for New York City banks is 13 per cent, and the Board can fix the figure at 26 per cent, or at any point between that and 13.

Accordingly, the Board may permit commercial banks to increase loans and investments merely by lowering the percentage, and can force them to reduce loans and investments merely by raising the percentage.

The "Dear-Money" Policy

When the Board acts to halt inflation, it follows what is known as a "dear-money" policy. This means that it increases the cost and reduces the supply of money.

The Board raises the discount rate, forbids the making of certain loans, reduces the amount of Reserve bank deposits, and increases the reserve percentage of commercial banks. The result of these actions, or of any one of them, is to reduce the stream of money that circulates between ourselves as consumers and ourselves as producers.

In prosperous times, there is always danger that the supply of money will be increased to the point of causing inflation — a supply out of proportion to our output of goods and services. Commercial banks are able and eager to lend money, and have almost unlimited opportunities to make good loans and investments. Active markets and firm prices for products give assurance that loans

[37]

for productive purposes will be paid when due.

Prospective high employment indicates that consumer borrowers will meet their obligations. Rising stock prices give safety to collateral loans. Real-estate loans are liquid. And firm bond prices offer sound opportunities for investment.

Under these conditions, our mechanism for creating money is bound in time to work faster than our machinery for producing goods and services. Then inflation will surely occur — unless the Board restrains our commercial banks in the creation of money.

In using the dear-money policy to achieve this purpose, the Board uses *deflation* as a means of preventing inflation. By reducing the stream of circulating money, the Board causes the income of consumers to fall, and thereby diminishes their ability to spend and to invest.

Demand is decreased and prices weaken. The results are a declining price level, an increase in unemployment, and a curtailment of production —

[38   ]

all of which constitute what we call deflation. In short, the Board avoids a rise by causing a fall in the price level.

The Effects upon Business

When the Board adopts a dear-money policy, the effects upon the planning of businessmen are profound and far-reaching. Even before the Board takes action, a statement of its intention is enough for commercial banks to warn businessmen that, for an indefinite time, there will no longer be a plentiful supply of money.

What that means in business and in the security markets we know by long experience, and we hasten to protect ourselves as best we can. These periods are times of business restraint and recession. Caution and anxiety replace confidence and enterprise. The outlook is for less buying, less opportunity to make profits. The supply of money is scarce and uncertain, and its cost relatively high.

Even if they can, farmers, manufacturers and merchants do not borrow to take full advantage of seasonal opportunities, for fear that loans cannot be extended if the need arises. Consumers' credit is reduced. There is much less occasion for plant and equipment expansion. And money, the energizing force of our economic life, flows slowly and at a low level through the channels of agriculture, commerce and industry.

It becomes good business to postpone purchases, reduce inventories, curtail production, delay capital expenditures and reduce commitments for borrowed money. Experience teaches us that this is the way to conserve our strength and be ready for the revival of industry and agriculture that will come after the end of dear-money policy.

Business leaders act immediately upon notice of impending dear money, and in a few months they are followed by the less wise. Soon liquidation becomes general, and about six months after the announcement, production of machinery, equipment and other capital goods declines.

Further, the advent of dear money starts a downward spiral in the security markets. Higher interest rates automatically cause lower prices for stocks and bonds. These falling prices, plus the scarcity of money, cause banks to cut their security loans, thereby bringing selling pressure on the markets. This gives us the downward spiral: declining prices cause bank loans to be reduced, which in turn causes further declines in security prices, which is followed by still further reductions in bank loans.

In view of these profound effects upon our business planning and upon our national economy, why does the Board use dear money as a device for preventing inflation? Why does it reduce the supply of money when there is no reduction in the activities of our economy? For what purpose does it control the lending of money by commercial banks? Just what does our Federal Government seek to accomplish by monetary manipulation?

These are questions of crucial importance to every American today. They have a direct bearing upon the security and welfare of all of us, in all walks of life. In fact, it can truthfully be said that upon a public understanding of these questions depends the survival of our system of competitive enterprise.

Dear Money Is Not Necessary

Let us start with the fact that it is *not* necessary for the Board to use dear money as its means of preventing inflation. All that is needed is to restrain the commercial banks from creating too much money in relation to goods and services — that is to say, enough money to cause a rise in the general price level. And this may readily be done merely by exercising control over the banks' required reserves.

For example, with our money supply today of 164 billions, the Board can keep the banks within that limit by restricting Reserve bank deposits to a total that prevents the banks from creating more than that amount, until more is required by increased production of goods and services.

In other words, to prevent inflation, the Board can merely hold undiminished the existing supply of money, and is *not* required to force a reduction of the amount in use. Why, then, does the Board from time to time pursue the dear-money policy, setting in motion the chain reaction which slows our productive activities?

The reason is simply this: the Board uses dear money as a means of controlling our willingness and ability to spend, save and invest. The Board, as we shall see, is an important part of the mechanism which has been set up in Washington to supervise and direct the economic life of the American people.

Although the Board makes much public talk about its efforts to prevent inflation, its primary purpose is to manipulate the supply, availability

[43]

and cost of money in order to regulate public spending, saving and investing. This statement may be hard to accept, but it is a fact, nevertheless. To understand it fully, we must take a brief look at the history of economic thought and monetary management.

V

Washington Takes Control

MONETARY MANAGEMENT as it exists today did not begin to take shape until after our Federal Reserve System was established in 1913. Prior to that time, monetary authorities failed to realize that the creation of money could be controlled by regulating loans and investments of commercial banks.

What happened in the United States before 1913 can be told briefly. The Federal Government had always had the power to regulate our supply of money, but until 1863, it exercised authority over little more than coinage. In that year, the Government gained control of paper money by the passage of the National Bank Act.

From this time onward, State banks were prevented by taxation from issuing notes, and the power to create paper bills was given to the newly established National banks. At the same time, Congress began to control deposit money, but only to the extent of requiring National banks to hold cash reserves against deposits.

In starting our management of money in 1913, the main intent of Congress was to solve a basic problem which arises from the use of deposits as money: i.e., while deposits are payable on demand, bank assets consist largely of notes with future maturities.

The Federal Reserve legislation followed the report in 1912 of the National Monetary Commission, created by Congress in 1908. The panic of 1907 had made clear once more that periodically, our banking system became paralyzed: banks found themselves unable to meet depositors' demands for cash, or to provide money urgently needed by industry, commerce and agriculture.

Accordingly, the chief aim of the Reserve Act was to enable banks to supply currency to depositors and still be able to make loans for production. Congress created twelve privately owned Reserve banks to act as banks for the commercial banks which deal with the public.

They are located in Boston, New York, Philadelphia, Richmond, Atlanta, Cleveland, Chicago, St. Louis, Minneapolis, Kansas City, Dallas and San Francisco. National banks are required to be members of the Reserve System, while State banks are permitted to join.

The Act gives the Reserve banks three great functions: to provide member banks with currency; to lend member banks money; and to carry deposits for their account.

As originally established, each Reserve bank was mainly an independent institution, with far-reaching authority to pursue its policies in its specific area. The Federal Reserve Board in Washington enjoyed little more than advisory powers, its chief function being to co-ordinate action among the twelve regional banks.

Financing World War I

During World War I, which began soon after the twelve Reserve banks were created, it became clear that each could bring about an increase in the money supply of the United States. Throughout the war years, and immediately afterward, the Reserve banks, by creating three billion in Reserve deposits, enabled our commercial banks to provide the Government with more than fifteen billion, by means of loans and investments.

That is how the Treasury was able to finance the war under the slogan "Borrow and Buy." It was the Reserve banks which made it possible for the American people to borrow the money required for the great Liberty Loan and Victory Bond drives.

In the wartime use of their powers, the twelve Reserve banks had no trouble in following a common course of action. Naturally, they did what they could to help the Government win the war. But when peace came, the officials faced a real problem in the fact that each of the banks possessed master monetary powers. And, as each began to increase or decrease our money supply, it was apparent that the System needed a national board with far more than mere advisory and co-ordinating powers.

The first step toward setting up centralized authority was taken by the Reserve banks themselves. In 1922, they formed a committee to bring about common action among the banks in regard to their control of our money supply. At that time, the head of a Reserve bank was called governor; and in 1922, a Committee of Governors was set up to co-ordinate the investing powers of the twelve banks. This group consisted of five governors, elected by the twelve governors at their annual meeting.

The second step was taken by the Board the following year. Ingeniously, it adopted an expedient by which the Board and the twelve Reserve banks would jointly supervise the banks' powers of investment. The Board formed a five-man committee of its own, empowered to control investing activities. And it appointed to this group the five governors who comprised the Committee of Governors elected by the Reserve banks in the previous year!

The third and final step toward centralized control was taken by Congress in 1935, when it created the Board of Governors of the Federal Reserve System. This called for a radical and almost complete reorganization of the whole System.

The independence of the twelve regional banks was ended, the name and functions of the Board were changed, and there was set up in this country a monetary and banking authority with powers such as those exercised by the Bank of England, the Bank of France, and other central banks abroad.

Today, the Board of Governors is a Federal agency that does exactly what its name implies —

it governs all the activities of the twelve regional banks and the 7000 commercial banks which comprise the Reserve System. These seven Presidential appointees have far-reaching control over the regional banks.

For instance, the chairman of the board of each Reserve bank, and its president and first vice-president are either appointed by, or must be approved by, the Board. And salaries of all officers and employees of each bank are also subject to Board approval.

In fact, the twelve Reserve banks today are little more than regional branches, carrying out the national monetary and banking policies formulated by the Board in Washington.

Keynes and His Ideas

STRANGE AS IT MAY SEEM, nowhere in the Reserve Act or in any amendment is the Board given an objective to follow as it increases or decreases our money supply. Congress has never told Reserve officials precisely what to do with their master powers. On the contrary, Congress has left to the officials themselves the responsibility of formulating their own policies.

In developing its plans, the Board has acted in accordance with the prevailing views of the economic profession — a profession which is currently divided into two major groups. Both groups, however, advocate regulating the supply, availability and cost of money in order to influence the willingness and ability of our people to spend, save and invest.

The first group comprise the followers of the late John Maynard Keynes, the British economist who believed in what amounts to State management of our economic life. The second group are the proponents of what is called a "Mixed Economy" — a plan under which Government planning is expected to give the American people the "best" in free enterprise.

The belief of these professional economists that our individual freedom in the use of money should be restrained is based upon the notion that in no other way can we maintain a high level of production and employment. They regard Government planning, direction and assistance as the only means to avoid or even greatly to moderate our periodic booms and depressions. And in this connection, Keynes proved to be one of the most influential men of our times, by his great success in putting over the idea that money management should be aimed at regulating the rate of investment in order to control the action of the people.

The Keynes idea, as set forth in his book, *The General Theory of Employment, Interest and Money,* is that the secret to prosperity is State supervision of what he called "the individual's propensity to consume and his inducement to invest." This was his way of saying that the Government should usurp some of our freedom of decision in the use of money.

The way in which the Board of Governors of the Federal Reserve is managing money in the United States today is essentially the same as that advocated by Keynes and now in effect in Great Britain.

Control by the State

Keynes contended at great length that, in our economic life, his program of money management was necessary to sustain high employment. According to his theories, Government planning and supervision of investment are required so that the capital goods and construction industries can operate at the rates needed for continuous prosperity.

He also advocated State compensation for the failures of free enterprise, and his way of managing money is an important part of the State control that he and his followers regard as vital to our economic welfare. Other parts of the program are these:

1. Government expenditures for public works, urban development, public health and other social programs.
2. Progressive income and inheritance taxation.
3. Deficit spending, and forced individual savings by means of deferred income payments.
4. In general, Governmental management of investments, with State activities compensating for inadequate savings and investment by individuals.

In presenting his theories, Keynes misled the economic profession into believing that the consumer and the investor are capricious in their use of money, and hence must be controlled. However, neither he nor any of his followers have provided monetary officials with a realistic, practical standard for determining *how* to exercise this control, or *when* to accelerate — or retard — the rate of spending and investing.

Keynes based his argument upon a proposition that fails to fit with economic facts. It is *not* true that under competitive enterprise we are unable to save and invest at the rate required for full production and employment. As a matter of fact, as pointed out earlier, businessmen under the guidance of prices and profits organize our productive activities in the right proportions generally for supplying goods and services.

Flexible adjustment between saving and investment is provided by bank loans because more than 30 per cent of our production is financed by bank credit. Business enterprises readily increase or decrease their borrowings to conform to the availability of savings. The extent to which accounts receivable, inventories and other quick assets are used as a basis for bank loans is a line that easily shifts one way or the other.

Actually, it is our practice year in and year out to spend most of our income, and to save less than 5 per cent. Both our rate of saving and of investment increase when the money supply is rising and, with a time lag, decrease when it is falling. The fluctuations that have occurred from time to time in the percentage of income invested or saved are traceable to increases and decreases that have taken place in the amount of money in circulation.

For example, the period from 1921 to 1929 was one of high savings, increasing standards of living, and generally full employment. This trend had a short-term correction in 1923, and was beginning to have a similar one in 1929, when it was brought to a disastrous close by mismanagement of our money supply by the Federal Reserve banks.

Mismanagement in 1937 was an important cause of low levels of capital-goods activity in 1938, offset later by increased expenditures for military supplies. Again in 1948 and early 1949, mismanagement by the Board brought sharply lower levels of activity.

Even though Keynes wrote extensively on fiscal subjects, he failed to take account of the effect upon consumer and business planning of the great ups and downs that have always occurred in the supply, availability and cost of money.

He recognized that the supply, availability and cost of money influence business activity, and that central bank actions affect both short and long-term interest rates. But having perceived this much, he did not pursue the fundamental problem. He concerned himself mainly with the effects upon interest rates of changes in bank credit. He hoped to stabilize investment and employment by means of fluctuations in long-term interest rates. He visualized a control policy which would cause the proportion of income spent for consumers' goods and services to change with changes in the interest rate.

Keynes failed, however, to explore the kind of

money management that is directed toward providing the people in a growing economy with funds needed for conducting their own affairs. Each year, for stability of production, price and employment, they require more money than the year before.

This is due, among other things, to population and production increases, to technological advances and improvements in the standards of living, and to increases in the amount of our money supply that is set aside for use in adversity and old age. But to that kind of monetary management, Keynes never gave his attention.

Theories vs. Facts

Why did Keynes fail in this respect?

In the first place, along with many other professional economists, he sought to learn economic truths by the process of reasoning and theoretical analysis, rather than by observing the actual facts of life. Indeed, much of classical economics has been developed from the beginning as a deductive science like metaphysics, instead of as an inductive science like chemistry, in which theories are derived from known facts.

Secondly, Keynes did not have an open mind when he conceived his ideas. For many years in his early life, he believed and taught the theories of the so-called classical economists, who analyzed our economic life as though we lived in a world of barter, where money was merely a convenient means of exchange. Later, when Keynes gave his attention to the subject of money management, his mind was too preoccupied with earlier views to permit realistic examination and study.

The Board of Governors of the Federal Reserve System is now following in the path which Keynes set forth, despite the fact that his project involves the steady growth of State management and control of economic life. How the supply, availability and cost of our money is regulated as a means of supervising the willingness and ability of the people to spend, to save and to invest, is fully set forth in numerous books and articles.*

By shifting back and forth between dear money and easy money, the Board is steadily weakening our system of competitive enterprise, and progressively helping to set up in the United States the other parts of the Keynesian program.

For twenty years we have been replacing competitive enterprise with a way of life that differs from the socialism of Great Britain only to this extent: over there, they are moving toward both Government ownership and Government control; over here, we have been moving toward a condition where we may still have private ownership — but only in a Government-controlled economy.

The chief instrument of this policy is the Federal

* Among them are two authoritative books by Dr. E. A. Goldenweiser, who had a leading part in developing the policies of the Board: *Monetary Management,* and *American Monetary Policy;* the booklet *The Federal Reserve System, Its Purposes and Functions,* issued by the Board itself; the book *Banking Studies,* and the pamphlet series, *Postwar Economic Studies,* written by staff members; and such standard textbooks as *Economics,* by Professor Paul A. Samuelson of the Massachusetts Institute of Technology.

Reserve Board in Washington, the very core of the large group of Government agencies that are now engaged in the huge task described as making free enterprise "work better," but which is in reality the setting up of an ever-growing system of Government control, disguised under the euphemistic title of "planned economy."

V I I

The "Mixed-Economy" Myth

Many economists who do not support the full Keynesian program nevertheless favor the Keynesian kind of money management. Vaguely they think that somehow or other, at some future time, we can devise a scheme of stopping midway the growth of a Government-controlled economy.

They believe that it is desirable, even feasible, to have a "mixed economy" — one that is planned and directed by Government officials *and* by the people themselves as they engage in productive activities. Or, to put it another way, they think it is possible to have both the competitive system of a free society and the regulation by Washington of our spending, saving and investing.

This belief in a "mixed economy" exists only because professional economists do not understand the operation of our productive machinery with its three elements of circulating money, changing prices, and fluctuating profit and loss. They still refuse to analyze the actual facts of our economic life and, in their process of seeking knowledge by reason and deduction, they have not yet understood how we produce in competitive enterprise under the guidance of a price-and-profit mechanism.

Nowhere in all economic literature is there a comprehensive, factual discussion of the effects upon business planning of changes in the supply, availability and cost of money; of the effects of price control upon our knowledge of supply and demand, upon our method of accumulating in the consumers' price the aggregate cost of production, upon our distribution of available goods and services, upon our opportunity as buyers to direct the course of economic life, and upon our ability as businessmen to regulate production.

Nowhere is there a comprehensive, factual discussion of the effect of profit control, by taxation or otherwise, upon the incentive to use labor, tools and money for productive purposes, upon the accumulation of funds for providing more and better tools, upon the formation and use of capital where needed to create what buyers want, and upon the placing of production and distribution in the hands of efficient personnel.

Unfortunately, professional economists, with few exceptions, do not seem to realize that Government direction of economic life, by whatever method, means giving up our price-and-profit mechanism as a guide to production. And they are not aware that when we do this, we must necessarily abandon our system of competitive enterprise.

Why are they blind to these facts?

On the one hand, they overlook the fact that Government officials cannot be guided by our price-and-profit mechanism — for they are *not* engaged in businesses that depend upon profits for survival.

Only individual businessmen and private companies can do their planning by observing changing prices and noting the effects of these upon their own prospective profits.

On the other hand, when the Government interferes with price and profit fluctuations, our mechanism does not function as a reliable guide for business planning. No longer do price changes indicate corresponding changes in supply and demand, or in costs of production; no longer do profit fluctuations indicate relative opportunities of producing what buyers want to purchase.

Moreover, even the best professional economists have not sufficiently examined the effects of monetary manipulation upon business planning to know that, in a free society, it is not possible to stabilize production by alternately increasing and decreasing the quantity and cost of money. They fail to understand that these ups and downs, by their effects upon the price-and-profit mechanism, bring delayed effects which lead to great surges in employment and production, and consequently they are unaware that it is impossible for the monetary authority to stimulate or retard production at will.

Actually, when the Board of Governors of the Federal Reserve makes money hard to get, it sets in motion deflationary forces that continue for more than six months, regardless of any action that the Board may take meanwhile. At least for this period of time, new orders are reduced, production is decreased and unemployment is increased. That is why the Board cannot moderately retard or quickly stimulate our productive activities.

Bank Credit and Business

Although it may come as a surprise to many readers, it is a fact *that more than 30 per cent of all American business is conducted with money borrowed from banks.* Few enterprises have enough capital and long-term debt to finance their own activities. The general practice is to rely upon banks for a substantial part of the capital needed for inventory purchases, for customer credit, and for peaks of seasonal business.

Further, almost all enterprises, except very small ones, are conducted under the protection of available bank credit. Many risks that otherwise would not be taken are incurred because bank loans are available to give protection from disaster, should events not turn out as expected.

Consequently, when the Reserve Board starts a dear-money policy, businessmen throughout the United States, upon the advice of their bankers, begin at once to curtail purchases, reduce inventories, postpone capital expenditures, and restrict general activities. Accordingly there is a drop in orders — a drop that gets bigger and bigger as it extends from retailer to wholesaler to manufacturer and to the supplier of raw materials.

If the retailer, say, cuts back 10 per cent, the wholesaler may cut back 20, since he not only gets less business from the retailer but has his own purchases and inventory to reduce. The manufacturer in turn may cut his order by as much as 40 per cent. Thus, almost simultaneously, the action by the Board in Washington affects virtually the entire business structure of our country.

The drop in orders is soon followed by a general falling off in production. Then comes a cutting of corporate dividends, and less personal use of profits from unincorporated businesses. With less money to spend and with less job security, consumers restrict their buying, particularly of durable goods. This puts further pressure upon retailers, whole-salers and manufacturers to reduce their activities.

Another reason why monetary manipulation cannot stabilize production is that Government officials can force us to use *less* money, but they cannot force us to use *more*. When they reduce the supply, we are unable to use funds that no longer exist; but when they increase the supply, we use the addition only as we see fit. We consider numer-ous factors besides the availability and cost of money before we decide to expand production, to increase spending, or to build new homes.

For example, we take account of "excess" capacity, of prospective prices and profits, and of future employment, income, expenses and taxes. In other words, dear money and easy money are *not* equally effective means of influencing our economic behavior.

The Reserve Board can do little about these public reactions to its zigzag methods of managing money. Our freedom to use money as we want is a fundamental liberty. And the long period of time required between planning and production in the capital goods and construction industries is a basic part of our production process.

Two Kinds of Profits

There is one more factor that must be considered when we examine our great waves of inventory buying and liquidation. That is the inescapable truth that in our profit economy there are two kinds of profits.

One kind results from the use of money, men and machines in producing and distributing goods and service. Only these profits are part of our mechanism of production, and perform the functions described in Chapter I.

But there are also profits of another and entirely different kind — those that arise merely from owning something on which the price goes up without fabrication, transportation, storage, insurance, merchandising or other improvement between the time of purchase and the time of sale. Profits of this kind are *not* helpful to America's productive machine; in fact, by encouraging speculation to take place, they actually interfere with its efficient operation.

When the Reserve Board alternates between dear money and easy money, it creates conditions that result in profits of this second kind — inventory profits and losses, as businessmen call them. The

[71]

reason is plain: such monetary manipulation affects the general price level.

For instance, when a dear-money policy is adopted, there is a tendency for prices to go down, and an opportunity to gain by reducing inventories, sometimes even to the point of exhaustion. Then, when the dear-money policy is reversed and an easy-money policy is pursued, the price level tends to go up, and manufacturers and merchants buy raw materials, semifinished and finished products, in order to make inventory profits.

Such profits, as pointed out before, are harmful to our system of competitive enterprise. Yet the Reserve Board, by using zigzag methods of monetary manipulation, creates the precise conditions that lead to great waves of inventory buying and liquidation. And these conditions, in turn, are a cause of periodic unemployment in the basic industries that support the American way of life.

VIII

The "Planned-Economy" Scheme

THE ECONOMISTS who advocate a "mixed economy" are doing more toward establishing Government control of economic life in the United States
than even the followers of Keynes. In the first place,
their support of the Keynesian brand of monetary
management makes them jointly responsible for
the great ups and downs in our stream of money.
And in the second, their proposals for planned
economy are more acceptable to the public than
the Keynes project for immediate and far-reaching
action.

The end results of both are the same, however,

since the planning of the mixed economists is increasingly interfering with the successful operation of our system of competitive enterprise. And the more they prevent the proper functioning of essential features of our productive machinery, such as the price-and-profit mechanism and the circulation of money, the more Government agencies are set up for the ostensible purpose of making free enterprise "work better."

Consequently, as a result of recurring unemployment caused by monetary mismanagement, the American people are coming to accept more and more Government spending for public works, for urban development, for unemployment insurance, for public-health programs, and for price-parity subsidies to farmers. More and more they condone heavy and progressive taxation of profits and incomes, despite the harmful effects of such taxation upon our productive ability.

In short, they are gradually being sold on the idea that it is necessary to have Government supervision of spending, saving and investing, together with Government regulation of production and distribution. Therefore, they are proceeding step by step toward a planned economy that is rapidly bringing to an end our system of competitive enterprise.

The powerful influence of the "planned economy" teachers on our education and political life is a dangerous and alarming development. Hence it is vitally important that the American people, especially businessmen and political leaders, understand two facts without delay:

1. The views of these economists have been formed without a comprehensive examination of the effects of monetary manipulation upon business planning.

2. Never have these economists proposed a definite and practical plan to stop midway, at some future time, the growth of their "mixed economy" into full Government control of all economic life.

[75]

Already we have lost much of the freedom that formerly allowed us to follow our own pursuits; to be rewarded for thrift, work and initiative; to go forward in the world according to ability; to save money for enterprise; to have the inducement to take risks; and to enjoy free choice in spending our money for the products of adventurous competitive enterprise.

What are the results of these restricting influences? Up to the present time, they are:

1. Development of new ideas and enterprises is restrained by taxes that prevent initial accumulation of capital and the setting up of a surplus as protection against later adversity.*

2. Work and endeavor are curtailed by taxes that take away the incentive of gain, and by restraints imposed by labor unions with Government assistance.

* It is true, however, that in the case of large and highly successful companies, research is stimulated by our heavy corporation taxes.

3. The value of insurance policies, savings accounts, and bond investments is progressively lowered by price-parity programs for farmers and cost-of-living wage increases for labor.

4. Competition is reduced by taxes on small business, by the heavy expense to small business of operating under intricate Government regulations, and by the capital gains that result from business consolidations.

Despite these crippling effects upon our national economic life, professional economists continue to support their scheme of a "planned economy." With few exceptions, they believe that it is impossible for business planning to sustain a high level of employment.

Unfortunately for the American people, these economists judge business planning by the results occurring under conditions when there was no monetary management whatever, or when there has been the type of management that in itself

[77]

causes a depression every time we get going in a period of prosperity.

Before 1863, we had "wildcat" bank notes and little control of deposit money. Between that date and 1913, we had an inelastic currency and periodic paralysis of our banking system. After that, we continued to have for some time an international gold standard that sacrificed domestic prosperity for the stability of foreign exchange. Now, for many years, we have had the method of management that shifts back and forth between dear money and easy money.

But never, at any time, has our Government managed money in a way that would make it possible for us, in an expanding economy, to have sustained prosperity under our system of competitive enterprise.

I X

The Management We Need

How can money be managed in a way that *does* permit business planning to bring about a sustained high level of production and employment?

In a free society like ours, there are two fundamental requirements of money management: (a) to provide a supply of money that is adequate but not excessive; and (b) to have monetary policies in accord with the fact that the course of economic life is directed by the people, as they do their buying and use their money in production.

To be adequate, our money supply must increase regularly from year to year, thus allowing a steady, even operation of the capital goods and construction industries. Only when we build new plants,

[79   ]

new equipment and new houses do we provide work for the men and women who earn their living in these industries and enable them to buy what other workers are ready to produce.

Moreover, only when we have activity in the capital goods and construction industries are we able to raise our standard of living and furnish work each year for the 800,000 boys and girls who, having completed their education, are looking for their first jobs. (The amount of money in the United States increased in each of the sixty years from 1892 to 1952, except in 1894, 1908, 1921, 1929–1933, 1938 and 1949 — and these were the years of deflation and depression.)

To have our money supply both adequate and not excessive, the creation of money by the commercial banks must be limited in a way that does not force them to reduce the supply in use. To prevent inflation, the monetary authority must *not* set in motion the forces of deflation, and thus cause businessmen to curtail purchases, reduce inventories and postpone capital expenditures. We cannot have sustained prosperity if, in order to prevent money from becoming excessive, we make the supply inadequate.

Unused Powers

For years, the Board of Governors of the Federal Reserve System has had ample power to provide the United States with an adequate but not excessive supply of money, yet, as we have seen, that has not been its policy. This ability of the Board to furnish us with all the money we require is proved by what was done during World Wars I and II.

In the former, the creation of three billion of Reserve bank deposits enabled the commercial banks to create for our use fifteen billions in circulating deposits; and in the latter, the creation of twenty-five billions of Reserve bank deposits made possible the creation of one hundred billions in circulating funds.

The powers of the Board to extinguish Reserve deposits, and to increase the percentage of required reserves, are more than ample to prevent the creation of too much money. In fact, these powers are used again and again to force commercial banks to reduce the supply of money, even though it takes more power to force a reduction than it does merely to restrain an increase.

Thus, it is plain that an inadequate supply of money is not due to the Board's inability to act, but to the use of its mighty powers to regulate our willingness and our ability to spend, save and invest.

In the face of this situation, is there any way in which the American people may be assured of an adequate, steady supply of money? There *is* a way — and it is a very simple and effective one.

It is only necessary for Congress to declare that the purpose of managing money is to provide the people with the amount they need to produce according to their ability and desire. What is required legally is merely the insertion in the Federal Reserve Act of a provision that should have been there from the beginning — a directive to the Board defining the objective toward which its great authority is to be used.

Barriers to Action

Two barriers stand in the way of such Congressional action. One is the strange fact that the economic profession has never advocated a monetary policy under which the people would be provided with an adequate but not excessive supply of money.

This road block, however, can readily be handled by a brief Congressional investigation. Such an inquiry would make clear the following facts to the public and to Congress:

Two hundred years ago, at the start of the science of economics, attention was concentrated upon production; money was regarded merely as a means of exchange — a device of convenience. As a result, there developed general agreement upon a funda-

[83   ]

mental but erroneous proposition that supply creates its own demand. Here is how the idea was expressed later by John Stuart Mill in his *Principles of Political Economy:*

What constitutes the means of payment for commodities is simply commodities. Each person's means of paying for the production of other people consists of those which he himself possesses. All sellers are inevitably, and by the meaning of the word, buyers. Could we suddenly double the productive powers of the country, we should double the supply of commodities in every market; but we should, by the same stroke, double the purchasing power. Everybody would bring a double demand as well as supply; everybody would be able to buy twice as much, because everyone would have twice as much to offer in exchange.

In commenting upon this erroneous notion in 1935, Keynes pointed out that many modern books on economics have assumed that the problem of production and employment can be worked out as though things are directly exchanged for each other, "with money introduced perfunctorily in a later chapter." He said that, originally, these conclusions may have been based upon a false analogy to some kind of simple Robinson Crusoe life.

Consequently, until recently, the view prevailed among economists who long have guided the course of American life that booms and depressions are the result mainly of unbalanced production — too much of this in relation to too little of that. In other words, bad planning by businessmen provided more of some products and less of others than the public desired to acquire.

Upon this foundation was built the planned-economy scheme discussed in an earlier chapter. Never was consideration given to the powerful and basic function of circulating money in our economic life. Manifestly, therefore, the failure of professional economists to advocate the constructive monetary policy proposed here should not block the way to Congressional action.

Confusion in Thinking

The other barrier to Congressional action is the confused public thinking about the causes of inflation and what must be done to eradicate them. This confusion exists among well-informed people as well as among the uninformed, and extends to leading businessmen, labor officials, newspapermen, commentators, educators, lawyers, clergymen, and members of Congress.

In part, the confused thinking is caused by the unrealistic way in which most professional economists talk about money; but chiefly it is due to the fact that our planned-economy advocates use public fear of inflation as a device for obtaining powers to direct the course of our economic life. They take advantage of the people's unawareness that the misuse of monetary power is a main factor in rapidly replacing our competitive-enterprise system with full-scale Government control.

Fear as a Tool

The fear of inflation is one of the most powerful forces circulating in America today. The American people, recalling what occurred not long ago in Germany, and more recently in China, see taking place here a creeping inflation which, by raising the price level substantially year after year, is steadily lowering the value of their dollars. Since the mid-1930's, the cost of living has increased so sharply that a dollar today buys less than a fifty-cent piece bought a few years ago.

The proponents of planned economy take advantage of this public fear when they ask that more power be given the Federal Reserve Board to regulate our use of money. They say that more effort is needed to protect us from inflation; but what they really want is more ability to manage our economic life.

Since the people do not know that reducing the supply and increasing the cost of money prevents

[87   ]

inflation only by causing unemployment and reduced production, they do not realize the connection
between this action and the great structure of Government agencies developing in Washington. When
they are assured by professional economists that
dear money is necessary to prevent inflation, they
blindly accept the consequences rather than take a
chance on destroying the value of the dollar.

As a matter of fact, the value of money has *never
been destroyed, anywhere at any time in all history,
except by an act of Government.* At such times, the
State prints vast and ever-increasing amounts of
paper money and causes banks to create larger and
larger amounts of deposit money (in the effort to
match mounting prices with colossal quantities of
purchasing power) until, finally, economic chaos
and collapse take place.

Against such a catastrophe, the Federal Reserve
Board could not give protection, no matter what vast
powers it might possess. The reason is simple: the
Board is a mere agency of the Government, and

[88   ]

could never be expected to control the State itself. On the contrary, whenever our Government engages in inflation, the Board is the chief agency for accomplishing the purpose, as we know from recent experience.

To prevent wild inflation, the American people must rely entirely upon their own common sense and strength of character. As a nation, they must not seek hurriedly to consume more than they produce, or permit their Government to spend money that is not obtained either by taxes or by loans that transfer existing money from the people to the State.

The Vicious Spiral

The creeping rise in our price level is due chiefly to the wage and parity-price policies of the Government. With the aid of Government pressure, and with the powers established by Federal statute, the big labor unions are forcing round after round of wage increases that push industrial prices upward. Meanwhile, the Government purchases farm products for the purpose of raising farm prices to what is known as "parity." The result is a spiral of inflation: higher prices cause higher wages, which in turn cause still higher prices.

This spiral exists only because the Reserve Board allows the money supply to increase. And no matter what powers are obtained for the Board, it can prevent this kind of inflation only during the period that it causes unemployment and loss of production, and shortly thereafter.

The reason is that, when the monetary pressure is removed and recovery is allowed to take place, prices rapidly return to the level which the authorities tried to reduce. Then the inflationary spiral becomes active all over again, since its causes are unaffected by monetary action.

There is one way, and only one, to clear up our confused thinking and misunderstanding about inflation. That is for leading businessmen, labor leaders, newspapermen, commentators, educators, lawyers, clergymen and members of Congress to inform themselves about the simple facts of inflation. Only then will we have the leadership needed to develop public opinion, and force prompt and constructive action from Congress.

X

The Facts About Inflation

IN EVERYDAY LANGUAGE, inflation means any rise in the cost of living, no matter what the cause. As far as the public is concerned, inflation exists whenever the value of the dollar goes down, whether this is due to an oversupply of money or to any of the other numerous factors which determine how much buyers obtain for the money they spend.

Inflation that is due to an oversupply of money is the result either of Government action in creating money by printing and bank borrowing, or of the creation of money by the people themselves through commercial bank loans and investments.

Among the nonmonetary factors that initiate or contribute to inflation are:

1. Advances in the wage level without corresponding increases in output or offsetting decreases in unit labor costs.
2. Advances in the price level resulting from Government purchases for the purpose of raising prices, or from corporation and income taxes that cause higher prices as a result of higher costs.
3. Higher price levels caused by reduction in output due to feather-bedding and other labor restrictions upon work, and by monopolies and general price agreements, such as the ill-fated NRA of the early 1930's.
4. Higher price levels due to Government price controls, restrictions upon use of materials, regulations relating to production, and other Federal interferences with supply and demand and the productive machinery of competitive enterprise.

Now, what can be done to prevent the various types of inflation? As for monetary inflation resulting from Government action, the only solution, as

[93   ]

has already been pointed out, is for the people to restrain the Government by combining their common sense with the power of the ballot.

As for inflation caused by the people themselves through commercial bank loans and investments, the only solution is for the Government, through the Federal Reserve Board, to restrain these banks from making loans and investments that create too much money in relation to goods and services.

As for inflation caused by nonmonetary factors, the solution in each case is to get rid of the cause. Take, for example, a wage-price spiral. To avoid this, we must abandon the policy of raising wages to meet advances in the cost of living, and halt the purchase of farm products for the purpose of raising prices. Otherwise, to prevent inflation in these cases, we must suffer unemployment and loss of production.

We must relate wage increases to reductions in unit costs, and let the market, in orderly fashion, determine the prices for farm products. This is the only way to safeguard the purchasing power of insurance policies, savings-bank deposits, pensions, Government and other bonds, and all other forms of fixed obligations and incomes.

And so it should be with other factors responsible for inflation: in each instance we must locate and get rid of the cause itself. It is a disastrous mistake to think that monetary action is a simple and easy method of escaping the consequences of inflationary spirals, taxation and fiscal policies, and of Government and other controls that interfere with our productive machinery.

Facing the facts is the only way that we can force Congress to resist the campaigns of pressure groups, as each group seeks to gain buying power at the expense of beneficiaries, homeowners, bank depositors, white-collar workers, and 45,000,000 American housewives.

When, in response to enlightened public opinion, Congress defines the purpose of managing money in the United States, recognition at last will be given to the fact that in our system of competitive enterprise, it is a function of the State to make available an adequate but not excessive supply of money. Then, for the first time, our monetary policies will be in line with the fundamental truth that economic life in our country is directed by the actions of 158,000,000 people as they decide what to buy, what to produce, how much to save, and how much to invest.

Aiding the Younger Generation

With an adequate supply of money available, the younger generation will see to it that the stream of circulating funds grows larger every year. They will accomplish this with their ever-recurring, ever-increasing demand for the means to obtain ownership and control of our economic facilities, as youth takes over from old age.

Young farmers and businessmen are ready borrowers to establish themselves in agriculture, industry, trade and commerce. Young people in the process of building and furnishing their homes, in acquiring the necessities and conveniences of life, are always eager to get the benefits today of their earnings of tomorrow. At the same time, the money borrowed and used by these young people offsets the funds withdrawn from circulation and set aside for the security of old age.

The commercial banks of the United States are effectively organized and equipped for providing money when it is needed for the growth of small businesses and the development of production and distribution. There are 14,000 of these banks throughout the country, each an integral part of our system of competitive enterprise. And, in every community, they offer opportunities to people of integrity, ability and initiative, who want to better themselves and get ahead in the world.

A Science of Forecasting

As WE HAVE already pointed out, it should be a function of the Federal Reserve Board to determine *when* to restrain the commercial banks and thus prevent the creation of an excessive supply of money. But — has the Board available all the information it needs to make such decisions?

The answer is yes. The information is supplied by recent developments in the field of economics. New methods are being used to examine the facts and measure the forces of economic life. At last, economics can be a science like physics and chemistry, where conclusions are reached by observing facts, and no longer an area of knowledge, like metaphysics and philosophy, where conclusions are evolved by reasoning, and where it is possible to have almost as many theories as there are economists.

Although these methods have been in use for little more than twenty years, experts today provide accurate and comprehensive information about what is happening in our current economic life, and can scientifically predict the course for years ahead. Already they have proved the vital fact that our people have precise, well-established habits in spending, saving and investing money.

These scientists are able to tell in advance how we will use increases in the national dollar-income; what and how much we will buy for our own use; and when and at what rate we will build new tools and equipment for expansion of production. When they foresee an increase in national income, they can forecast approximately how many radios, TV sets and washing machines we will buy; how many homes we will build; how much we will save; and how we will invest these savings.

[99]

In fact, these experts can predict with great accuracy, for a period of years ahead, how many cars of such types as Cadillac, Chrysler, Dodge and Chevrolet we are going to buy.

Today, the only peacetime uncertainty in these forecasts lies in calculating what the Federal Reserve Board will do about the stream of purchasing power. However, once the Board is directed to provide a supply of money that is adequate but not excessive, the economic scientists will be able to prepare reliable forecasts of the national dollar-income for years ahead, and to work out its relation to future production and distribution.

Instruments of Measurement

In reaching its decisions, the Federal Reserve Board will be guided primarily by index numbers, our economic instruments of measurement. With the skill and experience that we now possess in the making of index numbers, we have a quick and reliable means of measuring changes in economic conditions.

For example, we can observe today the changes that occur in the value of the dollar as accurately as a doctor can tell the changes in the temperature of a patient. Almost at the moment that the cost of living goes up (or stops going up), the fact can be learned with certainty by means of a comprehensive price index. Moreover, by the use of other index numbers properly constructed, the Board can promptly tell whether the advance is caused by the commercial banks, or by other factors such as wages, parity prices and taxes.

Higher prices from these other factors make it necessary to provide more money for the continuance of production and employment at existing levels. Consumers need larger incomes to buy the same number of units; producers require the use of more money for wages and material costs. As prices go up, the value of working capital goes down, and producers must borrow more from banks to continue doing the same amount of business.

Then the Board, in order to provide an adequate supply of money, must permit the commercial banks to increase loans and investments sufficiently to meet our requirements for production and distribution. But in following this course, the Board will publicly announce that monetary action is *not* the way to solve nonmonetary inflation.

On the contrary, attention will be called forcefully to the inflationary effects of cost-of-living wage increases, parity-price purchases, and tax programs that raise prices and lower the value of the dollar. As a result, the American people will come to realize that the only means of preventing such inflation is to bring public pressure upon Congress to halt inflationary farm, labor and taxation programs.

When the Board determines that a rise in the price level is due to monetary influences, it must take account of certain facts before exercising too much restraint on commercial bank loans and investments — facts about goods on order and in course of production, about the availability of labor, and about the extent of existing productive capacity. These elements may indicate that supply will soon catch up with demand.

Changing the Discount Rate

If the Board uses increases in the discount rate as a method of restricting commercial bank loans, great care must be taken not to set in motion the forces of deflation. The rate changes must not stimulate inventory liquidation or accumulation, cause uneven operation of the capital goods and construction industries, or bring about upward or downward spirals in security prices.

Only a slight change should be made at any one time, and this mainly to indicate an intention of using, if necessary, controls over reserve deposits and percentage requirements. Also, the Board must watch closely the effect of rate change upon the placing of orders by businessmen. If orders drop

[103   ]

sharply, indicating that the course of business planning is being reversed, the Board should take corrective action at once.

Whenever the Board restrains the creation of money, it should announce that as soon as the price level ceases rising, as a result of too much money, additions to the supply will take place again. And if the discount rate has been increased, the Board should state specifically that it will be reduced once the difficulty has been corrected. Then businessmen will not expect a prolonged period of declining prices, with later opportunities of making inventory profits when prices advance.

With little opportunity for inventory speculation, and no monetary reason for making basic changes in development plans, the short period of restraint should cause little if any interference with stable production and employment.

A Blow at Bureaucracy

There, in brief outline, is an escalator instead of a roller-coaster way of managing our money — a way to end the great fluctuations in purchasing power that are caused by huge increases and decreases in the stream of circulating money. With this kind of money management, we should be able readily, with no more than a thirty-hour work week, to double our output of goods and services. Then all Americans who are able and willing to work can live in health, comfort and security.

Lastly, this kind of money management will dispose of the one persuasive argument in favor of a planned economy in the United States — the argument that such an economy is essential if we are to have a sustained high level of production and employment. By managing our money to maintain a healthy, effective system of competitive enterprise, we will rid this country of an ever-expanding Federal bureaucracy, which is constantly seeking to widen its economic and political control over our daily lives.

XII

Peace and Prosperity

IN THIS CONCLUDING CHAPTER, the authors would like to summarize their opinions regarding three questions which affect the future welfare of every American:

1. What are our potential standards of living if, from here onward, we have an adequate but not excessive supply of money in competitive enterprise?

2. What are the facts concerning the current effects upon business of the Government's "planned economy" method of managing money?

3. How has Washington used America's defense program as a means of accelerating State control of our economic life?

With wise monetary management, how much we produce in the future will depend largely upon our desire for leisure. So far as our productive ability is concerned, there is practically no limit to what the American people can produce with their knowledge of mass production and technological research. Any doubts about that were settled by our accomplishments during World War II.

On the basis of these facts, it is reasonable to expect that as a result of continuous high employment, use of better tools, development of more efficient power-driven machinery, creation of new synthetic materials, and the steady, regular expansion of our productive facilities, we can be producing virtually as much as we want within the next five to ten years.

To most people, the very possibility of such rapid progress will seem incredible. But this is only because few persons are familiar with the extent and reliability of the knowledge which economic scientists are already supplying to American businessmen — knowledge that enables them to make long-range plans for development and expansion.

Once the Government provides the right kind of monetary management, each businessman in his own self-interest will *have* to make such long-range plans. He will know what to expect in the years ahead, and the man who uses initiative and energy in getting ready for prospective demand will prosper at the expense of his laggard competitors.

Conditions will be quite different from those which prevailed under the dear-money method of management. For no longer will it be wise for businessmen to wait until after the "next depression" before enlarging their productive capacity because of increased consumer demand.

Moreover, wise money management will give us a result of world-wide importance: the United States will become a genuine good neighbor to other nations, since our stream of purchasing power will match our stream of products. Once our national income permits us to purchase our national output, then we can buy from abroad the equivalent of our foreign sales.

No longer will so-called "overproduction" force us to seek prosperity by means of a "favorable" balance of trade — our way of exporting unemployment. Up to now, in our endeavor to maintain employment at home, we have caused widespread unemployment abroad. But when we buy from other nations the equivalent of what we sell, our neighbors and ourselves will contribute to each other's prosperity in mutually profitable trade.

Current Effects of Monetary Policy

Throughout much of 1951 and 1952, the Board of Governors of the Federal Reserve System pursued a dear-money policy. The result was that the long-term interest rate rose by more than 10 per cent, and the short-term rate by more than 50 per cent. During the last nine months of 1951 and the first nine months of 1952, merchants and distributors throughout the consumers' goods industries reduced their orders and liquidated portions of their inventories. By the summer of 1952, many consumers' goods plants were operating at rates well below capacity, and some had shut down.

During this time, despite the advance in interest rates, the total money supply was permitted to rise by more than 5 per cent. Thus, by its actions, the Board caused the supply of goods to decrease, and enabled the amount of purchasing power to increase. It is not surprising, therefore, that consumers' prices reached a new high in December 1952.

However, the rise in prices was due mostly to factors other than money, such as the wage-price policies, inflationary tax programs, and Government interference with the machinery of production. Yet, in justifying their dear-money policy, Government officials made the usual statements that in order to prevent inflation, it was necessary to increase the cost of money. Under these conditions, the familiar pattern of reduced production, unemployment and a lower standard of living will inexorably develop.

Meanwhile, public fear of inflation is being used by Washington as a device for obtaining more powers of centralized economic control. And, as part of the same program, Government officials are greatly exaggerating the burden of our defense production. The people are told that our productive machinery is operating at capacity, and that defense requirements are so vast that price and material controls are required if the Government is to get what is needed.

In actuality, American business could readily have taken in stride the 15 per cent additional burden placed upon our productive ability by defense requirements — a relatively small undertaking in comparison to what was achieved during World War II. But despite this demonstrable fact, the planned-economy advocates have used Communist aggression as a means of acquiring vast

[111]

peacetime controls over the economic life of the American people.

These price and material controls are not only unnecessary, but they seriously impair our ability to produce. They interfere with the price and profit mechanism of our industrial machinery, and defeat their own purpose by increasing civilian demand and reducing total supply.

Take, for example, the case of steel. Our people were told that the supply of steel was much less than required. Ostensibly this was true for a time, since the Government's control action temporarily caused enormous quantities to be hoarded or otherwise withheld from normal use. It is now apparent, however, that without controls, the Government could have filled its requirements as needed and still have had enough left over for the demands of business.

Time Is Running Out

For the economic welfare of our free society, there is much our Government can do besides providing the right kind of monetary management. We need a system of taxation which, insofar as is possible, comprises merely a transfer of purchasing power to the Government — not an interference with production. We need general laws setting forth in clear and definite language the rules and regulations for fair and competitive conduct of free enterprise. And we need farm policies, labor policies, tariff policies and social policies which are conceived and executed in the interest of *all* the people.

If we act wisely in managing our money, all these objectives may be achieved without great difficulty. But we must act soon, or nothing else will matter. If we continue to manage money as we have done during the past twenty years, the free society of the United States can survive only for a relatively short time.

[113   ]

With a strong and healthy economic life, we can retain our freedom as individuals and protect ourselves from any aggressor in a world-wide struggle for survival. We can develop the military power we need, furnish arms to other nations, assist them in gaining economic strength to defend themselves and, at the same time, raise our own standard of living. All this *can* be done with the prodigious productive power latent in our free, competitive-enterprise system.

Actually, planned economy and free enterprise are two entirely different ways of living. They are based upon directly opposite concepts of life: one maintains that people are better off when told what to do, the other that they are better off when they decide for themselves what to do.

In planned economy, Government officials make the decisions which direct the daily course of economic life; in free enterprise, individual men and women make their own decisions.

Planned economy is Government direction of

economic life. The State formulates plans for the production and distribution of goods and services, and uses coercive powers to carry these plans into effect. Government boards make plans and Government officials make decisions extending into every field of industrial, commercial, financial and agricultural activity. Controls may be exercised over prices, profits, income, capital formation, credit, competition, and over the use of raw materials, labor, power, transportation and finished products.

The individual is restrained whenever and to whatever extent the State-planners see fit. Economic freedom exists only at the will of the Government.

In contrast, wise and realistic management of money will provide a basis for the development of a great program of expansion under free enterprise as an alternative to planned economy. A new way will be opened to solve the problems that gave birth to the Keynesian and mixed-economy schemes of governmental controls.

By proceeding on this new road, we shall no longer run the risk of defeating Communism by our military and diplomatic efforts, only to find that we have set up a totalitarian government of our own. On the contrary, by following a course of positive action, we can as a good neighbor lead the world to peace by the strength of our example as a happy, prosperous and free nation.